What is War?
What is Peace?

The war in the Gulf has ended,
but there remain many questions
about war and peace.

This book, developed with kids
just like you, is designed to answer
some of your questions.

The war in the Persian Gulf is only
the world's most recent war. What
have we learned from wars in the past?
How can we stop them from
happening again?

The more you know, the more
you can do to make peace.

What is War?
What is Peace?

50 QUESTIONS AND ANSWERS FOR KIDS

by Richard Rabinowitz

President, American History Workshop

Illustrated by Paul Meisel

A Byron Preiss Book

AN AVON CAMELOT BOOK

WHAT IS WAR? WHAT IS PEACE? is an original publication of Avon
Books. This work has never before appeared in book form.

AVON BOOKS
A division of
The Hearst Corporation
105 Madison Avenue
New York, New York 10016

Special thanks to Ellen Krieger, our editor at Avon Books

Editor: Gillian Bucky
Assistant Editor: Kathy Huck
Book design by Michael Goode
Cover design by Stephen Brenninkmeyer
Cover illustration by Paul Meisel

First Avon Camelot Printing: May 1991

"Camelot World" is a trademark of Byron Preiss Visual Publications, Inc.

CAMELOT TRADEMARK REG. U.S. PAT. OFF. AND IN OTHER
COUNTRIES, MARCA REGISTRADA, HECHO EN U.S.A.

Printed in the U.S.A.

OPM 10 9 8 7 6 5 4 3 2 1

Contents

Introduction

When a war starts, it's hard to get away from it. Everyone is talking about it. It's on the news. Flags and yellow ribbons are everywhere. It's difficult not to think about it. War is scary.

Until the war in the Persian Gulf, you may have thought that war was like a video game. Using buttons and a joystick, you blast little enemy warriors on a screen. If you miss, all you have to do is press a button and *blip*, you create new good guys, new targets, and new bad guys to zap.

But war isn't like that. People die in wars, and there is no way to bring them back. The pictures in the newspapers and on TV during the war in the Persian Gulf showed how serious it really is. There were pictures of soldiers, warships, jet fighters, guns, missile launchers, tanks, and bunkers. There were interviews with President Bush and Saddam Hussein. There were oil fields on fire and Scud and Patriot missiles lighting up the night sky. There were explosions. There were reporters looking pretty nervous. There were prisoners of war. There were pictures of wounded soldiers.

The fighting in the Persian Gulf has made all of us think more about war.

War is very complicated and can be hard to understand. For this reason, it's important to ask questions and look for answers.

What is war? Who invented war? How much does a war cost? Why do some wars last for a few days while others go on for years? Why do people go to war? Do all wars start the same way? How do you know when a war is over?

This book was written to help answer questions you have about war and about peace. Some questions are very hard to answer. Some have no answers. Some questions are very personal, and you must decide what the answers are for yourself.

INTRODUCTION

Allied missiles light up the night sky in Baghdad, Iraq.

The best way to understand is to ask questions. When you ask questions, your brain and your heart are talking. And this is much better than being angry or scared and letting your fists do the talking.

So never stop asking questions. It helps make peace.

The Dog and Cat Game

Here is something for you to think about. Imagine
that you are in charge of a cat and a dog. This cat and
dog are at war. How would you try to keep the two
from fighting? Draw a picture showing your idea.
Here are some ideas other kids have had:

- Put a leash on the cat and a leash on the dog and
  keep them separated.

- Put a lion in the room to keep the peace.

- Give the cat and the dog so many toys and treats
  that they don't notice each other.

- Raise them as a kitten and a puppy to love each
  other.

- Put a wall between the dog and the cat so they can't
  even see each other.

- Put the dog in a cage.

- Teach the dog and the cat not to fight.

- Dogs and cats always fight. Let them.

- Put all their food in one dish. Then they'll have to
  learn to cooperate.

- Give the cat away.

- Give the dog away.

- Teach the cat karate so the fight will be even.

- Make them sit down at the United Nations.

Chapter 1

How Does War Begin?

War is a very difficult, very confusing subject. There are many questions that seem to lead to even more questions. So let's start at the beginning.

Who invented war, anyway?

No one actually invented war. War has been around for as long as people have been around. There are cave paintings by prehistoric artists which date back to the Stone Age showing people fighting with spears and rocks.

But what is war?

The dictionary says that it is an open armed (meaning weapons are involved) conflict (meaning a fight) between nations. A nation is

a group of people who have something in com-
mon or are connected in some way. They may
be connected because they live in the same
country, follow the same leader, or share a reli-
gion. A nation can be big, like the United
States, or small, like Costa Rica. A nation can
have boundaries, like a country. A nation can
also be a group (or tribe) of people without ties
to a specific country.

Why do nations fight?

Nations have fought for the things they need to survive, such as water, food, and land. Leaders of nations have fought for power, control, and strength. Nations have fought over religious and racial differences. Nations have fought because they believe they are right and the other nations are wrong.

* For example, let's say you belong to a nation of Plerbles. You are proud to be a Plerble. Plerbles wear purple socks and live peacefully by the river. You are loyal to King Plop, ruler of Plerbia. One day, the river mysteriously dries up. King Plop asks you to find out what the problem is. You walk along the riverbank until you come to the land of the Flurfs. The Flurfs are hard to understand because they don't speak Plerbian. They hate socks and mistrust people who wear them. You see that they have built a dam that has dried up the river. King Plop asks the king of the Flurfs to take down the dam and share the water. The king of the Flurfs refuses. And so King Plop feels he must do what he has to do to win back the water his people need to survive.

WHAT IS WAR? WHAT IS PEACE?

Do any other animals, beside human beings, have wars?

Ants do. Ants live in very complex societies. If you've ever had an ant farm, you know what I mean. Each ant is born to do a certain job and they do it for their whole lives. Some are workers, some take care of the babies, and some are warriors. Ants fight because it is instinctive for them to do so and for some of the same reasons people do—food, territory, power, and control.

Do people fight because of their instincts, too?

People have very strong instincts. When you see someone being a bully, your instincts might tell you to help the person being bullied. Or your instincts might tell you to run away in case the bully decides to pick on you. One instinct human beings share is a need to be with other human beings. It makes sense. People feel more secure in groups. In a group, people can work cooperatively. If your group is in trouble, your instincts will probably tell you to try and protect the group. There

are times when those kinds of instincts (to protect what is important) lead people to argue or even fight.

Do all wars start with messengers going back and forth?

Many do. The messengers are called diplomats. They try to prevent war by using words rather than weapons. They negotiate.

When words don't work, do people start fighting?

Not always, but in many cases that is what happens. The leaders will try to prevent war by talking, but when negotiations aren't working, the leader of a nation might decide to give up and declare war.

Once the fighting starts, can nations stop and the leaders go back to talking?

That can happen. Sometimes, nations at war are like two dogs who bark and growl at each other when there is a fence between them. If you took down the fence, they'd realize they don't really want to hurt each other or be hurt, so they quiet down and walk away. This can happen between nations at war. Sometimes, a third nation or a committee of nations (like the United Nations) will be asked to help settle things. The people who represent their countries at the United Nations are kind of super-diplomats. They try to solve the little arguments before they become big fights. This doesn't always work. Diplomats might talk for days before someone decides there has been no progress. Then the diplomats or the leaders of the country they represent might call off the negotiations and refuse to talk any more. This is called a stalemate. If nothing more can be accomplished with words, the leaders bring in the generals, who speak with actions. Usually one nation decides not to talk anymore and makes the first move.

What kind of first move? What is considered an act of war?

An act of war can be just about anything. Sometimes a nation just says, "you are my enemy and we declare war," then orders its soldiers to start shooting. Sometimes a nation doesn't have a strong or organized army. Such a nation might use an act of terrorism, like blowing up an airplane or taking hostages. Sometimes a nation will use a blockade, which means trying to defeat the enemy by blocking their roads and cutting off supplies and lines of communication.

Sometimes an army will just cross the border and take over (or occupy) another nation. That's what Saddam Hussein, the leader of Iraq, did. In August 1990, he ordered his army to invade Kuwait. He claimed that Kuwait was no longer a separate country. Instead, he said, Kuwait was now a part of

HOW DOES WAR BEGIN?

A boy watches President Bush announce the launching of the Gulf War air attack.

Iraq. The leader of Kuwait, the emir, escaped, but many Kuwaitis were killed, held hostage, or terrorized. It's hard to say whether or not Hussein meant this to be an act of war. Sometimes the beginnings of war are hard to pin down.

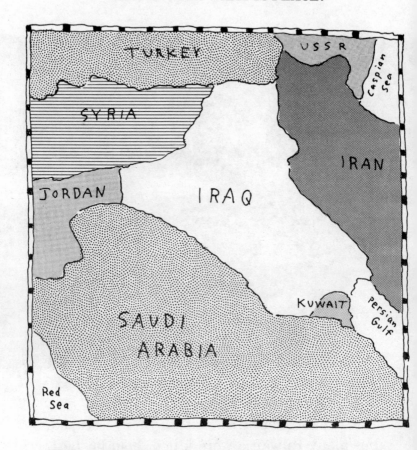

Why did Saddam Hussein pick on Kuwait?

There were many reasons why Kuwait was an attractive target for Hussein. Kuwait is a very wealthy country because of its oil fields. Long ago, Kuwait and Iraq were part of the same country, and Hussein claimed that by invading Kuwait he was merely returning the land to its rightful owner. Iraq had been at war with another neighbor, Iran, from 1980 to 1988. The Iraqi army had lost a lot of equipment and spent a lot of money. Hussein wanted to rebuild his army fast. He needed to buy more planes, tanks, missiles, and supplies. Kuwait's wealth could help him do this. In addition, Kuwait sits right on the water—the Persian Gulf. Hussein wanted to control a bigger piece of the coastline of the Persian Gulf so he could have his own seaport for exporting and importing all types of goods, including oil. It's also a good military strategy for a nation to have access to the sea: It means you can have a navy. With military strength and control over Kuwait, Hussein believed that he could become a powerful leader in the Middle East. He would win the respect of his people and of Iraq's allies. He could sell some of the oil for high prices. And if he could take over Kuwait, then maybe he could take over other countries, too.

Why did we get involved with Kuwait?

We sent our troops over to protect Saudi Arabia, a neighboring country, from Iraq after Iraq invaded Kuwait. We tried to negotiate with the Iraqi leaders. The United Nations warned Iraq to get out of Kuwait. The diplomats of the United Nations passed resolutions, which are like a list of demands and rules to follow. They told Iraq to pull out of Kuwait or face punishment. But Iraq didn't listen to these warnings. The nations that belong to the United Nations decided that if Iraq could not be trusted to behave responsibly, then it could no longer enjoy the privileges of trade with its member countries. The United Nations decided to impose sanctions, which meant that it was forbidden for countries that belonged to the United Nations to send anything into Iraq. No weapons, no machines, no food, and no medicine. And no country was allowed to buy anything that Iraq was trying to sell. The idea was to make Iraq weak economically and force Saddam Hussein to give up.

Workers clean up after Iraqi Scud missiles destroyed many buildings and homes in Tel Aviv, Israel.

WHAT IS WAR? WHAT IS PEACE?

This worked—to a point. But this kind of strategy takes time, and the Iraqi army was destroying more of Kuwait each day. The United Nations and the United States finally gave Iraq an ultimatum: It had to agree to the resolutions and get out of Kuwait or be prepared to go to war with the allied forces.

The United States and allied forces were finally forced to go to war. First, beginning on January 16, 1991, they started an air war. They bombed military posts and installations in Iraq and in occupied Kuwait for five weeks. The Iraqi army had been killing Kuwaitis and looting Kuwait's cities. They set fire to the Kuwaiti oil pumps. They dumped millions of gallons of oil into the Persian Gulf, causing a horrible tide of pollution. They kept firing Scud missiles at Israel and Saudi Arabia and threatened to use chemical weapons. On February 23, 1991, the United States and the allied forces sent ground troops into Kuwait. In a very quick ground war, Kuwait was liberated and most of the Iraqi army retreated into Iraq. One hundred hours after the ground war started, President Bush

HOW DOES WAR BEGIN?

Kuwaiti oil fields were set ablaze by Iraqi forces.

went on television to declare a cease-fire. The Iraqi generals finally agreed to the United Nations resolutions.

Why was Israel a target, anyway?

The leaders of Iraq and some other Arab nations have long considered the United States and Israel their biggest enemies. When the war started, Saddam Hussein thought that if he could get Israel involved by shooting missiles into the country, other Arab nations would support him. That might have made the conflict in Kuwait spread to other parts of the Middle East, and many more people would have been killed on all sides. But instead of becoming involved in the conflict, the Israeli leaders decided to stay out of the fighting and let the United States and the coalition forces handle the war.

Have there been other leaders like Saddam Hussein?

Throughout history, there have been leaders who wanted power, respect, and wealth, and would do anything to get them, including going to war. One such leader was Adolf Hitler of Germany. In World War II, another war in which the United States took part, the German dictator attacked one European nation after another. He wanted to create a German Empire that would extend around the world. More than 20 million people, both soldiers and civilians, died in World War II.

Was Saddam Hussein crazy?

That's hard to say. He wanted to be one of the most powerful leaders in the Middle East. Power is a strange thing. Some people, when they get some power, want more. Power becomes like a drug and they can't stop wanting it. They'd sacrifice anything and everything to get it.

Are the Iraqi people our enemies?

No. The acts of a leader or of a group of leaders do not always represent the feelings, hopes, and wishes of all the people. President Bush said many times during the war that the Iraqi people were not our enemies. Sometimes the people of a nation follow their leader because they are scared not to. When a war is over, it's time to rebuild. If you hold onto the idea that someone is your enemy and will always be your enemy, you are keeping the war alive.

Chapter 2

How War Works: Strategy and Tactics

War is complicated. Like a game of chess, it has rules, but not everyone follows them. It's kind of like a video game, but in war, decisions have aftereffects. It's like football, but war doesn't stop when someone gets hurt on the field or when the quarter is over. Let's talk about how a war works.

What other kinds of wars has the United States fought in?

There are different kinds of war. For example, the United States fought for independence from England in the American Revolution. France was our ally. (In fact, France and the United States have been allies

Proclaiming independence from British rule, the colonists initiated the American Revolution.

ever since.) The American Revolution started in 1775 in the towns of Lexington and Concord, in Massachusetts, and ended when the British admitted defeat in 1781. About 25,000 people died, and many homes and farms in the South and in New England were destroyed. (Other nations have fought wars for independence, too. In this century, for example, Indonesia won its freedom from the Dutch and Algeria won its freedom from the French.)

The Civil War (which is also called the War between the States) lasted from 1861 to 1865. A civil war is a conflict between two groups who are a part of the same country. In other words, Americans fought Americans. It was long and bloody. Out of all the suffering and sacrifice came the end of slavery and the survival of the Union.

The United States is not the only country to have had a civil war. Since 1900, there have been civil wars in Spain, China, Lebanon, and Nigeria. In many ways, a civil war is the most horrible kind of war. It sets families, friends, and neighbors fighting against one another.

We also came to the defense of our allies in World War I and World War II. These wars took place mainly in Europe and the Pacific.

When war starts, do two sides just start firing away?

No. A war is a very complicated thing. Each side in a war has a strategy. It's the big plan you have worked out to beat your enemy.

Facts about Past American Wars

War	How Long It Lasted	How Many Americans Involved	How Many Americans Died*
American Revolution	1776 to 1783	not available	around 25,000
War of 1812	1812 to 1815	286,000	over 2,000
Mexican War	1846 to 1848	79,000	13,000
Civil War	1861 to 1865	2,000,000	620,000
Spanish–American War	1898	300,000	2,400
World War I	1914 to 1918 (U.S. entered 1917)	5,000,000	117,000
World War II	1939 to 1945 (U.S. entered 1941)	16,000,000	400,000
Korean War	1950 to 1953	6,000,000	54,000
Vietnam War	1964 to 1973	9,000,000	58,000
Gulf War	1991	500,000	300

* These numbers are approximate and include deaths that occurred not only in battles, but from disease, starvation, and other war-related causes.

Of course, both sides want to win. But the strategy is the plan for how to win. And a good strategy is one in which the enemy is defeated without a lot of people getting killed. Sometimes, a strategy can be simply to frighten the other side into surrendering without a shot.

Many, many years ago, when knights went into battle, the strategy was usually simple. Knights wore armor and carried flags so that everyone knew which side they were on. They would meet in an open place, like a field, and charge at one another on horseback. They used weapons such as spears, lances, axes, and bows and arrows. They fought until one side ran away, was killed, was captured, or surrendered.

Strategies today are usually more complex. The leaders of the nations at war develop a strategy with their military leaders and advisors. The president of the United States consults with his cabinet, members of the Congress, diplomats, and generals (the word "strategy" actually comes from an ancient Greek word meaning "general").

These leaders decide what their goals are and then plot a strategy to reach their goals. In the case of the war in the Persian Gulf, President Bush had several goals. He wanted to liberate Kuwait. He wanted to destroy Saddam Hussein's power in the Middle East. And he wanted make sure that the world would continue to be able to buy oil in the Middle East.

What happens once you've decided on your goals?

The next step is to find out as much as you can about the enemy. You'll want to know how big their armies are and where their armies are. You'll want to know what kind of weapons your enemy has and how many. You'll want to know how they supply their armies, where the roads are, and where the airports are. You want to know what their weaknesses are and what their strengths are.

There are many ways to get this information. Armies will send spies and scouts behind enemy lines. It's also possible to "monitor" (listen in on) telephone calls and radio broadcasts. Modern technology has made it possible for satellites in space to take close-up pictures of airfields, truck convoys, and other things happening on the ground.

How do military leaders decide what to do in a war?

That is what the strategy is for—it is the plan everyone follows. As in a game of

A World War II U.S. commander plans his strategy against the enemy.

football, there is an offensive strategy for attacking and a defensive strategy for protecting yourself from attacks. In the Persian Gulf War, the United States and its allies worked on their strategy together. They called their strategy "Operation Desert Storm."

What was our strategy for the war in the Persian Gulf?

Diplomacy, trade sanctions, and warnings were not working. President Bush warned Saddam Hussein one last time: If he didn't obey the United Nations' resolutions and pull out of Kuwait by January 15, 1991, he should expect war. Hussein didn't leave Kuwait. President Bush and the allied commanders ordered Operation Desert Storm to begin on January 16. It started with a huge air war. American and allied planes flew thousands of sorties (missions) and dropped thousands of bombs on military targets in Iraq. They also bombed places in Kuwait where the Iraqi army was positioned.

*U.S. Marine F/A-18 Hornets fly over Kuwait on a
bombing mission of Iraq.*

WHAT IS WAR? WHAT IS PEACE?

Why was it a good strategy to begin with an air war?

In the case of the Persian Gulf War, starting out with an air war made sense. If you destroy the enemy's airfields and airports, how will he get his planes off the ground to fight back? If you destroy the command centers, how are the generals going to command their troops? If you bomb their roads and bridges, how are they going to transport weapons, food, and soldiers from place to place?

This strategy worked very well. When the ground war began, thousands of Iraqi soldiers were captured or surrendered within days. They were sick, hungry, and thirsty. Their supplies had been cut off by the heavy bombing.

Why wasn't it our strategy to just kill Saddam Hussein?

Although the United States and the allies felt that Saddam Hussein was responsible for the war, it was decided not to make him a target. Even though deception is used in war and everyone knows it, there are some unwritten rules. One of these rules is that it is unac-

President Lincoln addresses a group of officers during the Civil War. The president is commander in chief of the armed forces.

ceptable to single out the leader of another country to be killed. Also, President Bush was hoping that the Iraqi people would take away Saddam Hussein's power themselves when they saw what was happening to their country.

Who says when a war can actually start?

The president, as the commander in chief of all the armed forces, can order troops into battle. But our Constitution states that he cannot start a war until Congress declares it.

When war starts, how do all the individual soldiers know what to do?

Behind the strategy, the plan, are the men and women who are in charge. They make up the chain of command. You probably have a kind of chain of command in your family. Say your mother asks you to pick up a pretzel from the floor. You tell your little sister to do it. She tells the dog to eat it. That's a chain of command.

HOW WAR WORKS

In the armed services, the president is at the top of the chain. He gives orders to the next link in the chain. In the army, this would be the generals. They then give orders to the next link in the chain—the colonels. They then give the orders to the next link in the chain—the majors. Orders continue on down the line to the privates.

This way, every soldier is taught the importance of following the chain of command. Every soldier listens to and follows the orders of his or her senior officer. If there weren't a chain of command, there would be no one in charge. Soldiers wouldn't know what to do. There could be no strategy.

How did we tell the generals of our allies who didn't speak English what to do?

All of our allies fought in their own units. We didn't mix all the soldiers up into one big army. That would have been a mess. Each country had different weapons and different equipment. Each unit had translators who spoke English and other languages.

How do all these people actually make a war happen?

Remember that the generals follow the strategy for the war. Wars are made up of battles. Battles are specific fights. In battles, tactics are used. Tactics are parts of the big plan. For example, the strategy the United States and its allies used in the Persian Gulf War was to start out with an air war and weaken the Iraqi army by bombing military sites all over Iraq. The targets chosen, the number of planes used, the types of bombs used, and the time of day the planes flew are examples of the tactics that were used.

People use strategies and tactics every day to accomplish their plans. Say your strategy is to finish your book report over the weekend. Your tactic might be to go to the library on Saturday and then write the report on Sunday. When you sit down to do the work, you'll make sure you have the proper supplies.

The Saudi Arabian desert calls for a unique set of ground tactics.

Do the tactics change?

Tactics sometimes change from minute to minute. It depends on whether or not they are working. Let's say your tanks are in position but the enemy has lined up missile launchers right where the tanks are supposed to go. So, the tank commander asks the commander of the air force to bomb the enemy missile launchers before they begin to fire.

How do you figure out what the tactics will be?

There are many things involved in planning tactics. The geography of the battle-field makes a big difference in choosing tactics. A battle in the desert will use different tactics from a battle in the jungle. Weather will also affect tactics. The number of soldiers each side has, the types of weapons involved, and the amount of supplies you have are all considered when planning tactics.

With so many soldiers, how do they hear what's going on?

Before walkie-talkies, radios, and satellites were invented, armies used different ways to communicate during a battle. Coded messages were sent by smoke signals, lanterns, drums, bugles, and flags. It's also possible to use the sun and a mirror: By reflecting the sun off a mirror, a soldier can flash a message in code to a friend. During the two world wars, pigeons were trained to fly

between two places with messages tied to their feet.

Do we still use these ways of communicating?

Yes. Modern armies still use some of these old-fashioned ways to send messages. Some soldiers are taught a special way to wave flags to make messages. They use a special language called "semaphore." Ships "talk" to one another using flags. Each flag stands for a letter in the alphabet. The flags can be strung together to make words.

Long ago, how did generals decide on tactics if they didn't always know what was going on?

During the Civil War, generals spent many hours on their horses. They galloped from one place to another. It was very tiring and very dangerous. Messengers were also used. But it took a long time for information to travel. It was hard to follow tactics because it was hard to know what was going on.

How do civilians know what is going on?

Until recently, they didn't. Information can travel only as fast as the way it's being sent. In the old days, that meant that news traveled with people walking or riding in stagecoaches or on horseback. Slow-moving ships took news across the oceans. News traveled very slowly. Sometimes it took months—even years—to find out what was going on. In 1815, during the final weeks of the War of 1812, the Battle of New Orleans took place. News traveled so slowly that none of the soldiers knew that they had fought the battle *after* a peace treaty had ended the war.

A field artist for a weekly magazine sketches a battle during the Civil War. Until recently, information during wartime traveled very slowly.

WHAT IS WAR? WHAT IS PEACE?

How did people learn about what was happening in World War II?

In World War II, people went to the movies to see "newsreels." (Television wasn't in homes yet.) Newsreels were short movies that showed what was happening around the world. But the news was still about what happened weeks before. Now we have telephones, telegraphs, videos, satellites, modern newspapers, radios, and televisions to help us report the news the second it happens. But even now, we are not always told what's going on. It's part of strategy. Sometimes it's best for some news not to get out right away, because if the enemy hears it it could put our soldiers in danger.

Did You Know That...

• The longest war in history lasted 115 years, from the year 1338 to the year 1453. It was called the "Hundred Years' War" and was fought between England and France.

• The shortest war lasted 38 minutes! It was between the United Kingdom and Zanzibar and lasted from 9:02 to 9:40 a.m. on August 27, 1896. It ended swiftly because Zanzibar surrendered right after the United Kingdom started its bombardment.

• Out of the past 5,000 years of the world's history, there have only been a total of 292 years when there hasn't been a war going on somewhere in the world.

• The oldest army in the world is the Swiss Guard in the Vatican City in Rome, Italy. It was organized before the year 1400.

• The tallest soldier of all time was Väinö Myllyrinne. He entered the Finnish army when he was 7 feet 3 inches tall and later grew to 8 feet 3 inches!

• The youngest soldier of all time, Marshal Duke of Caxias, entered the Brazilian army in 1808 when he was five years old and became a military hero and statesman.

• The longest march in military history was made by a large group of Chinese Communists in 1934-5 when they walked 6,000 miles to get from one part of China to another. It took them a whole year to do it and so they called it the Long March. In that year they crossed 18 mountain ranges and 6 major rivers.

Chapter 3

The Armed Forces

There are several parts that make up the armed services of the United States. They are the army, the navy, the air force, the Marine Corps, the Coast Guard, and the Merchant Marine. Each part or branch has its own chain of command leading up to the commander in chief, the president. During a war, all the branches work together and follow the same strategy.

The Army

Different sections of the army do different jobs. There are the infantry, the armored units, and the artillery. The largest number of soldiers are in the infantry. Infantry soldiers are nicknamed "foot soldiers" because they do a lot of walking. They carry rifles (called M-16s)

An army tank clears a path for infantry units.

and are also equipped with grenades, machine guns, and small rockets that can be carried into battle and fired by one or two soldiers.

Soldiers in the armored units (who drive the tanks) and artillery help the soldiers in the infantry. They protect the foot soldiers by clearing a path for them as they go into battle. They fire cannons and rockets that are much larger than the weapons infantry soldiers carry. Some cannon shells and missiles can travel over 20 miles. They strike very deep behind the enemy's front lines.

The army also trains pilots to fly planes and helicopters. Some attack enemy positions. Some look for the enemy and for targets so the tanks will know where to aim their guns. Some take wounded soldiers to hospitals. Some take pictures of the landscape so the generals can plan tactics. Some are like flying buses, moving soldiers, supplies, and equipment from place to place.

There are all sorts of units (groups of soldiers) that do other jobs. Some deal with communications and some with transporting soldiers, supplies, and equipment. Some units are made up of engineers. They do things like build bridges and destroy minefields. Some units take care of the laundry and cook. There are lots of details that have to be taken care of if an army is to run smoothly. Tactics and strategies can get all messed up if someone

forgets to order the three Bs: beans, bullets, and Bandaids.

The soldiers are moved around in helicopters, planes, and ships. On land, they travel in trucks or in special vehicles that look like tanks, called "armored personnel vehicles." Sometimes they are parachuted into position.

There were lots of tanks used in the war in the Persian Gulf. This was part of the strategy. Tanks are built to move quickly over any-thing. They can go through water and up and down steep hills. Unlike trucks, they don't get stuck in sand or mud. They don't need to go on roads. If anything gets in its way, a tank will just mow it down. They can fire their big guns while moving fast. Like a turtle's shell, their outside is built to protect them. Tanks are very solid. They weigh as much as forty cars.

The Air Force

Mostly, the air force flies planes. Every plane, such as the F-16 and F-111, has a pilot. In addition, every plane has an on-ground crew of about 16 soldiers to look after it. They have to keep the planes repaired, refueled, loaded with bombs, and ready to go.

Airplanes are sent out on many kinds of missions. Mostly, they are sent on bombing missions. They bomb targets that are impor-tant to the enemy's army. They try to destroy bridges, roads, airports, missile launchers, enemy airplanes, oil refineries, and factories where weapons are made. They try to stop enemy supply trucks. In ground battles, they

U.S. Air Force B-17s fly over Germany in a World War II bombing mission.

try to hit targets that are putting our soldiers or supplies in danger. Other missions are for surveillance (information gathering).

Airplanes protect other airplanes from enemy attacks. Some fighter planes fly just to defend bombers, tanks, and other fighter planes from enemy airplanes and anti-aircraft guns. Another way to protect airplanes is to keep them on navy ships called aircraft carriers.

The Navy

Just as there are special types of tanks and artillery units in the army, there are special kinds of ships in the navy. Each ship has a different job. They usually travel in groups to protect one another. That's a good defensive tactic. There are missile cruisers that fire missiles at targets on the sea, in the air, and on land. There are battleships that have 16-inch guns. These are very powerful weapons. There are ships that look for enemy submarines or for mines in the sea that could destroy other ships. And there are submarines that can fire torpedoes underwater. Some of the ships are like floating stores filled with food, weapons, and supplies. Some are hospital ships to take care of the sick and wounded.

The navy also has an air force. Navy planes (with names like Tomcats, Hornets, Intruders, and Hawkeyes) take off from and land on runways aboard ships. Each aircraft

A massive aircraft carrier transports planes to their military destinations.

carrier has about 85 planes. They are the largest ships on the sea. More than 5,000 sailors live on one aircraft carrier.

The Marine Corps

The Marine Corps does a combination of the kinds of jobs the army, navy, and air force do. Like the infantry, marines can carry rifles into battle. They have special equipment like the artillery. They use special ships to land on beaches. They have paratroopers (soldiers trained to use parachutes) and pilots, too. The marines are trained to fight anywhere.

Other Services

In the United States, there are the Coast Guard and the Merchant Marine. The Coast Guard rescues people on sinking ships or from planes that have crashed into the sea. It also patrols the home waters around the United States. The Merchant Marine consists of sailors on the ships that carry supplies in wartime.

Ranks in the Four Services

ARMY

Officers:
General (4-star)
Lieutenant General
  (3-star)
Major General (2-star)
Brigadier General (1-star)
Colonel
Lieutenant Colonel
Major
Captain
Lieutenant
1st Lieutenant

Enlisted:
Sergeant Major
Command Sergeant Major
Master Sergeant
1st Sergeant
Sergeant 1st Class
Staff Sergeant
Sergeant
Specialist
Corporal
Private 1st Class
Private

NAVY

Officers:
Admiral
Vice Admiral
Rear Admiral Upper Half
Rear Admiral Lower Half
Captain
Commander
Lieutenant Commander
Lieutenant
Lieutenant Junior Grade
Ensign

Enlisted:
Master Chief Petty Officer
Senior Chief Petty Officer
Chief Petty Officer
Petty Officer 1st Class
Petty Officer 2nd Class
Petty Officer 3rd Class
Seaman
Seaman Apprentice
Seaman Recruit

THE ARMED FORCES

MARINES

Officers:
General (4-star)
Lieutenant General
  (3-star)
Major General (2-star)
Brigadier General (1-star)
Colonel
Lieutenant Colonel
Major
Captain
1st Lieutenant
2nd Lieutenant

Enlisted:
Sergeant Major
Master Gunnery Sergeant
Master Sergeant
1st Sergeant
Gunnery Sergeant
Staff Sergeant
Sergeant
Corporal
Lance Corporal
Private 1st Class
Private

AIR FORCE:

Officers:
General (4-star)
Lieutenant General
  (3-star)
Major General (2-star)
Brigadier General (1-star)
Colonel
Lieutenant Colonel
Major
Captain
1st Lieutenant
2nd Lieutenant

Enlisted:
Chief Master Sergeant
Senior Master Sergeant
Master Sergeant
Technical Sergeant
Staff Sergeant
Sergeant
Senior Airman
Airman 1st Class
Airman
Airman Basic

Units of the Armed Services

ARMY AND MARINES

Unit	Components	Total Soldiers	Commanded by
Squad	———	9 to 12	Staff sergeant
Platoon	3 squads	about 30	Lieutenant
Company	3 or 4 platoons	100 to 130	Captain
Battalion	3 to 5 companies	500 to 750	Lieutenant Colonel
Brigade/ Regiment	2 to 5 battalions, plus support units	1,800 to 4,000	Colonel
Division	Normally 3 brigades, plus support units	11,000 to 17,000	Major General
Corps	2 or more divisions, plus support units	50,000 to 100,000	Lieutenant General

THE ARMED FORCES

AIR FORCE

Units	Components	Commanded by
Flight	11 to 15 pilots	————
Squadron	2 or more flights	Lieutenant Colonel
Wing	2 or more squadrons	Colonel
Group	2 or more wings	1, 2, or 3-star General
Air Division	2 wings	1-star General or Senior Colonel
Numbered Air Force	2 or more divisions	2 or 3-star General
Major Command	2 or more Air Forces	4-star General

★ ★

NAVY

(The navy does not have such clear-cut units. These are the three major groupings of ships in the navy.)

Type	Example	Contains
Aviation ships	aircraft carrier	up to 85 aircraft, 6,000 crew members
Undersea ships	submarine	nuclear missiles, 165 crew members
Surface ships	battleship	missiles, launchers, guns, 1,500 crew members

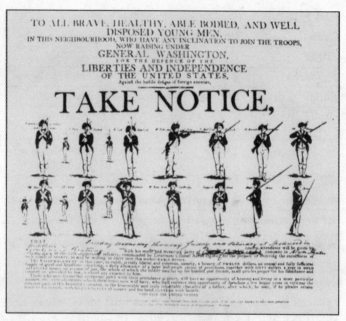

Posters are still a popular form of advertisement for army recruitment.

Chapter 4

A Day in the Life of a Soldier

Wars are fought by people. The men and women of the armed services are expected to do their jobs in dangerous times in faraway places. Let's talk about what it is to be a soldier.

How do you get to be a soldier?

There are several ways. Each branch of the armed forces has certain requirements. There are recruiting offices where you can go to fill out an application. This is called volunteering. A recruiting officer will tell you a little bit about basic training and what you should expect if you join.

In times of war, the government might decide to start a draft. This means that if you meet the requirements and you are healthy, you could be ordered to join the armed forces whether you wanted to or not. There was a draft in the 1940s for World War II and in the 1960s and 1970s for the Vietnam War. Right now, the United States doesn't have a draft law. Our volunteer armed forces seem to be working out well.

How old would you have to be to be drafted?

To have a draft, Congress would have to pass a new law, but it would probably not call up anyone under 18 years old.

Is there any way not to get drafted?

One way is to ask for a *deferment*. There are different kinds of deferments, such as being a student in college or having to take care of your family.

What happens in basic training?

You learn how to be a soldier. You learn your job. You learn about weapons. You learn about the chain of command and how to follow orders. You learn how to salute and how to wear your uniform. You do exercises to make

you stronger. You become familiar with the mental and physical discipline necessary to be a soldier. Basic training usually lasts between six and ten weeks. The amount of training you get depends upon the job you get.

How many American soldiers were in the war in the Persian Gulf?

At first, about 150,000 soldiers were sent. President Bush and the generals decided on a strategy to send more soldiers if they thought it was necessary. More soldiers were sent over after Iraq said it would not leave Kuwait. By the time the war actually started, there were about half a million soldiers there. That included soldiers from all the branches of the military.

How did all the soldiers and their equipment get there?

As the different units were called up and got their orders, they left their bases in the United States. Some soldiers already serving in Europe and the Middle East were also called up. Some traveled by ship, but most were flown over. Some of the trucks and tanks were transported along with the soldiers in planes. The really heavy equipment went over in ships.

British soldiers set up their equipment in preparation for an attack during World War II.

Who set up the army's camps?

There are soldiers who have the job of setting up camps. They figure out what has to be ordered and built. They order food, water,

Cost of Items Used in Operation Desert Storm and Number of Each Item Bought by the U.S. Military

One MRE: $4.00
Military purchased: 91 million (MRE stands for "Meal Ready to Eat." An MRE contains the same kinds of foods you can buy at the supermarket, like chicken, spaghetti, beef pot roast, chili, macaroni & cheese, and lasagna)

One pair of soldier's boots: $50.00
Military purchased: 1.4 million pairs

One pound of sugar: 40 cents
Military purchased: 7.16 million pounds

One pound of coffee: $1.40
Military purchased: 2.6 million pounds

One pair of cold-weather underwear: $10.40
Military purchased: 1.1 million pairs

One pair of goggles for sand, wind, and dust: $4.15
Military purchased: 376,000 pairs

One pair of soldier's pants: $15.50
Military purchased: 5 million pairs (factories manufactured 2,000 a day)

One pair of chemical protective gloves: $7.30
Military purchased: 175,000 pairs (they already had over 1.8 million pairs on hand)

tents, beds, extra clothing, and medical supplies. They set up telephone systems, garages to maintain the trucks and jeeps, hospitals, latrines (bathrooms), showers, and mess halls (cafeterias). They order weapons, ammunition, and fuel.

How did they know what to order?

They knew from experience and they had to do a lot of arithmetic. They knew there were 500,000 soldiers. Each soldier eats three meals a day. Multiply 500,000 by three and you get a million and a half meals. Every day! In the case of the Persian Gulf War, because it was hot and dry, they also knew the soldiers were going to need lots of extra water to drink—about three or four quarts for each person every day.

What do the soldiers do if the fighting hasn't started yet?

When they first arrive, the soldiers have to set up their base camps. It's like building a little city. They put up tents. They unpack equipment and get it set up. Then

they exercise and have target practice and keep their guns clean. This was hard in the desert because of the dust and the sand. Mostly, the soldiers wait.

Can soldiers have fun?

Soldiers can have fun when their work is finished and when their senior officer says it's okay. They can watch television, videos, or movies, play cards, play ball, write letters home, listen to music, or rest.

Where do they plug in their TVs?

The base camps in Saudi Arabia were connected to the Saudi electrical system. They

Free time in Saudi Arabia: a marines vs. navy touch football game.

also used generators, which are portable motors that run on gasoline and make electricity.

Do soldiers get tired of waiting?

Yes. Sometimes it's hard to wait around when you have been trained to do a job. Sometimes soldiers get lonely and homesick.

Can soldiers make telephone calls?

When the soldiers have free time, they are allowed to call home. They are not always allowed to talk for very long and are not always allowed to tell their family or friends where they are. (Remember, you don't want to risk letting your enemy know where you are!) Before the telephone was invented, soldiers had to rely on letters and often had to wait a long time to get them.

Which soldiers did most of the work when the war in the Persian Gulf started?

The pilots and their crews were very busy during the entire war. They flew sorties day and night for weeks.

What did the women soldiers do?

There are many women soldiers in the American armed forces. About six percent of the American soldiers sent to the Persian Gulf were women. But only men soldiers are sup-

A female marine carries her combat gear along with two bottles of water after arriving at a Saudi airbase.

posed to fight. It is a military law that women soldiers can only serve as "noncombatants." So while men pilots flew combat missions, women pilots flew other types of planes. Women worked as members of the ground crews, too. They loaded the bombs onto the planes and repaired the engines. Even though they were not doing the actual fighting, women soldiers did dangerous jobs in the Persian Gulf War. Several were captured as prisoners of war, and several were killed.

What can soldiers do if the other side uses chemical weapons or poison gas?

They can wear gas masks that will help them breathe until the wind blows the gas away. They can also wear protective uniforms and take special medicines. The United States and its allies knew that Iraq had these kinds of weapons and so they prepared themselves. Every soldier had a gas mask just in case.

A DAY IN THE LIFE OF A SOLDIER

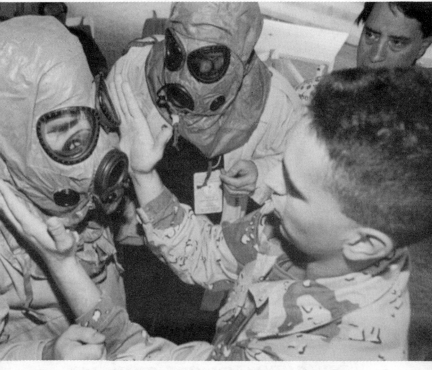

Gas masks were commonplace for soldiers and civilians during the Gulf War.

How is the gas sent?

The chemicals or gas can be sprayed from airplanes or put inside missiles (called warheads) and fired at the enemy like regular missiles.

Did American and allied soldiers have to wear the special uniform and gas masks all the time?

No. Because of radar and other modern equipment, it's possible to tell when enemy planes are coming. Sirens would go off and soldiers and civilians would have several minutes to get ready.

What about the soldiers who were in the desert and couldn't hear the sirens?

They got warnings by radio, and they kept chickens. Chickens were used as a kind of alarm. Chickens react to the gas before human beings do. So, if the chickens died, the soldiers knew to put on their gas masks—fast!

What happens when a soldier gets sick or hurt?

There are doctors, nurses, and hospitals (called "field hospitals") that travel with armies. There are also hospitals on board the large ships. The International Red Cross (an international organization that works to aid refugees, sick and wounded soldiers, and vic-

A DAY IN THE LIFE OF A SOLDIER

A World War II medic helps a wounded soldier.

tims of natural disasters) helps out, too. In addition, there are specially trained soldiers called "medics" who travel with the infantry during battle and give first aid until the soldiers can be taken to a field hospital. If a doctor in the field hospital thinks the problem is serious, then the soldier is flown out by helicopter or plane to a hospital in an allied country. Even during the Civil War, there were field hospitals and men and women who took care of wounded soldiers on the battlefield.

Is a wounded soldier sent home?

It depends on how serious the wound is. Some soldiers are able to get better and return to their units. Some are treated in field hospitals and then sent home to get better. Anyone who is wounded in battle gets a medal. It's called the Purple Heart.

What happens when a soldier is captured?

In war, soldiers are sometimes captured. Sometimes, pilots have to bail out of their planes when they are shot down flying over enemy territory. They become prisoners of war (or POWs). There are rules about what to do with POWs. Their names and serial numbers are sent to the International Red

Cross. That way, their families will know they are okay. POWs should be fed and given medical care if they need it. They cannot be hurt or made fun of. Doctors from the International Red Cross should be allowed to visit POWs to make sure they are being treated well. Unfortunately, some countries do not obey these rules.

What happens to POWs when the war is over?

They should be returned to their country as soon as possible.

What happens to soldiers who die in war?

The rules about POWs also apply to soldiers killed in battle. The bodies of soldiers killed in war should be treated with respect. There is a special cemetery near Washington, D.C., called the Arlington National Cemetery. It's for soldiers who have died in war. Not all soldiers are buried there. It's up to their families to decide.

How long does a battle last?

It depends. Battles can be over in minutes, a few hours, a few days, or even weeks. One of the longest battles of the American Revolution lasted a day. One of the longest, bloodiest battles of the Civil War lasted three days. That was at Gettysburg, and almost 50,000 soldiers died. The whole ground war in Iraq lasted only four days.

The war seemed to go on night and day. Do soldiers in battle get to rest?

Not a lot. Things move quickly and orders change quickly. That's why basic training is so important. The training and practice help to make the soldiers tough.

How does a soldier become a hero?

In a way, all soldiers are heroes. Soldiers are expected to be brave and do their jobs under all kinds of conditions. They leave their friends, families, and schools behind. They do very hard work. They work in teams and follow the chain of command. But some-

Soldiers rest on fold-out cots next to a tank in the Saudi Arabian desert during round-the-clock exercises.

times, individuals do very brave things or make personal sacrifices. They receive special medals for their heroism.

After the war is over, do soldiers have nightmares?

Some soldiers have scary experiences. They sometimes see things that are hard to forget. Being in the middle of a battle is very hard. There are explosions so loud you can't believe it. There is smoke and dust and confusion. Sometimes your friends are hurt or killed. Sometimes war itself is a nightmare.

So why does anyone want to become a soldier?

There are lots of reasons. There are many opportunities in the armed services. You can learn new things, meet people, make friends, and travel. You can get special training for certain types of jobs. You can get scholarships to help you go to college. You can learn about military traditions and about leadership and responsibility. But most of all, you can serve and help protect your country.

War and Peacetime Decorations and Medals

Medal of Honor: Given to soldiers who do something extremely brave and unselfish in battle, and who risk their life in the process.

Distinguished Service Cross, Distinguished Service Medal, and Silver Star: These different medals are given to soldiers for doing noble, brave, and unselfish things in battle.

Legion of Merit: Awarded to someone who shows exceptional behavior while performing an outstanding service in the war. This award goes to nonsoldiers, like doctors and nurses, as well as to soldiers.

Soldier's Medal, Airman's Medal, and Navy and Marine Corps Medal: These are peacetime medals, which means that they are given to soldiers who risk their lives while they are not in a war. For example, a soldier who saves someone from a burning building may earn this medal.

Army Commendation Medal: Often given to junior soldiers for heroism, achievement, and/or very good service.

A DAY IN THE LIFE OF A SOLDIER

Good Conduct Medal: Given to enlisted soldiers who have shown good behavior and loyalty, and who have done a good job while serving in the armed forces.

Purple Heart: A medal given to people who were wounded or killed while fighting in battle. This medal was created by George Washington in 1782 but was not awarded again until 1932.

Distinguished Civilian Service Award: This goes to people who work for the Department of Defense but who are not soldiers. They may be office administrators or clerks. It is the highest award that a civilian can receive.

Medal for Merit: An award given to civilians of either the United States or its allies for doing something very courageous or helpful in the war effort at home.

Medal of Freedom: This is the highest award that a civilian who does not work for the Department of Defense can receive. It is given to someone who does something to help protect the security and national interests of the United States and its allies, either in wartime or in a time of peace. In 1963, John F. Kennedy renamed it the **Presidential Medal of Freedom** and decided it should also be given to people who make very important contributions to world peace.

Chapter Five

The Home Front

Wars are not just fought on fields of battle. A war is like a raindrop in the middle of a lake. The ripples on the water reach all the way to the shores—all the way home.

Why do people hang flags everywhere when war starts?

A nation's flag is a powerful symbol. Showing the national flag is a sign that you are proud of your country and that you are proud of the people who are fighting the war. Flags also fly on special holidays like Veterans Day (when we honor the men and women who have been soldiers) and the Fourth of July (Independence Day), when people show their patriotic feelings.

Why does a war seem to make people more patriotic?

It might look that way. More flags appear when a war starts because people want to show their support for the country and the armed forces. When the country goes to war, people often have strong feelings. Some people are for the war. Some people are against it. People talk about it, watch the news, and even argue about it. Some people are neutral.

What is neutral?

Neutral means in the middle. If you are neutral in a war, it means you are not taking a side and not getting involved. People can be neutral and countries can be neutral. When World War I and World War II started, the United States tried to be neutral. But we didn't stay neutral. In World War I, we declared war after Germany sank some of our ships that were trying to cross the Atlantic Ocean. In World War II, Japan pulled us into the war by attacking Pearl Harbor, an American naval base in Hawaii.

Isn't it better to remain neutral and not get involved in a war?

Sometimes it's very hard not to get involved when one country attacks another. Say you or one of your allies is attacked. Nations have responsibilities to one another. Bigger, stronger nations sometimes try to protect smaller nations. Nations sometimes agree to help one another if there is a war. They have treaties. A treaty is a kind of contract between two countries or several countries. It explains what should happen if one of the nations that is a part of the treaty is attacked.

What happens if a nation isn't sure it wants to go to war?

The United States didn't want to get involved in World War II for many reasons. For one thing, World War I was still fresh in the minds of many Americans. So the country waited. Germany was invading a lot of little countries in Europe. They invaded France and were bombing England. But when Germany's ally, Japan, bombed the American naval base in Pearl Harbor, we could not remain neutral. In the case of the war in the Persian Gulf, the United States decided *not* to go to war when Iraq first invaded Kuwait. Instead, we agreed to follow the plan the United Nations drew up. We agreed to put an embargo on Iraq.

What is an embargo?

An embargo is a type of sanction. It is a set of rules that prevents a country from doing business with the rest of the world. In the case of Iraq, the countries that belong to the United Nations agreed not to sell anything to Iraq and not to buy anything from Iraq. The idea behind an embargo is to hurt a country's economy and force the leaders to give up before a war starts. Although the embargo and sanctions ordered by the United Nations weakened Iraq, Iraq refused to give up without a fight.

How do the leaders of a country find out what the people want to do?

There are lots of ways for people to let their government know what they are feeling and thinking. Americans phone and send letters to the president and to members of Congress. Some people go to marches, rallies, and demonstrations. Newspapers and television stations interview people and conduct surveys. They ask people their opinions and then write about the results.

Did people think that going to war with Iraq was the right thing to do?

Some people did and some people didn't. According to surveys, most American people felt that going to war with Iraq was the right thing to do. Most of the members of Congress agreed with President Bush's decision to start the war with Iraq. After the war, the surveys showed that most Americans thought that President Bush did a good job.

Can you be against the war but still be patriotic?

Yes. It is important for everyone to have an opinion about things as important as war and peace. Some people think that it isn't right to fight another country's war. Some people think there are more important wars to be fought right here in the United States—like the war on drugs or the war on poverty. Some people believe that peace is the only answer. Some people believe that war is never justified.

Peace marches and peace demonstrations are an important way to express an opinion. They are a good way to show other people how you feel.

What did people do at home when the Persian Gulf War started?

People talked a lot about the war and what it all meant. People read newspapers, listened to the radio, and watched television in order to know what was going on. A lot of people wore yellow ribbons on their clothes or

Demonstrators protest the Gulf War.

tied yellow ribbons to their front doors. Yellow ribbons are a symbol that shows that the friends and families of soldiers at war are thinking about them and waiting for them to come home safely. During World War II, a war in which we were directly involved for almost four years, people on the home front did lots of things. People saved pieces of metal to be recycled. People knitted socks for soldiers. Movie stars and famous singers volunteered to go to Europe and entertain the troops. Because so many men were in the armed forces, women and children did a lot of extra jobs to help out.

What happens if you don't want to fight in the war?

Participation in the armed services is done on a volunteer basis now. But during World War II and the Vietnam War, there was a draft. The government ordered all young men who were 18 years old to register for the draft. There wasn't a choice because it was the law.

For some people, fighting in a war is against their personal or religious beliefs. For them, fighting is wrong no matter what. These people still have to join the armed forces, but they will be given a job that doesn't involve fighting. They are called *conscientious objectors*. Some people don't believe in serving in the armed forces in any way. They might decide to leave the country and live somewhere else. Some 18-year-old men made this difficult choice during the Vietnam War. This war had gone on for a long time and was becoming more and more unpopular. Some people risked going to jail rather than fight. It's important to remember that everyone has the right to oppose the war.

It's very difficult to have someone you know or someone you love go to fight in a war. You worry about them and they worry about you. You wonder if they are okay and what they are doing. It's hard to know, sometimes, whether it's better to protest war or show your support for it. Some people support the troops but don't believe in the war.

How would we know what to do if a war started here?

We have been very fortunate. There hasn't been a military attack on the continental United States for 130 years. Wars take time to get started, and we would probably have many warnings. As we have seen, lots of things happen before a war begins. Diplomatic talk, embargoes, economic sanctions, United Nations resolutions, and other warnings are examples of what can happen before the actual fighting starts. Even so, we have a whole system called civil defense. Satellites, lasers, and radar will warn us if another country

British civilians take shelter in the London Underground (subway) during World War II.

decides to attack. In the cities, we have sirens that will warn people to be prepared for an attack and air-raid shelters to protect people just in case. There are special announcers who come on television and on the radio and tell civilians what to do.

What happens to a kid if his or her parents are soldiers at war?

When soldiers are ordered to go overseas, their families just keep on doing what they always do. It's hard when a mother or father is away. Many families stay on or near posts or bases. They are like military towns. At posts and bases, soldiers get special training and practice what they've learned. Some soldiers and their families live in apartments near the base. The military helps take care of a soldier's family when he or she is away.

The armed services try not to send both the mother and father if they can help it. But if both parents are needed, their kids are always taken care of. Some kids go to live with their grandparents, or their grandparents might come to live with them. Maybe an aunt and uncle or family friend will help out. It's very hard for kids when their parents are ordered to go somewhere else for a while. It's very hard for the parents to be separated from their kids, too. War is very, very hard to understand. Even if it's in a faraway place like Kuwait, it still affects so many people in so many ways all around the world. That's why, when we are at war, military people call the United States the "home front." They know the people at home are making sacrifices and are always involved in the war in some way, too.

Donations to Operation Desert Storm

One way in which citizens support their country during a war is by donating items to the armed forces. Items donated to American troops during the Gulf War varied from batteries to yoyos, and the donors themselves ranged from celebrities such as Paul Newman and Arnold Schwarzenegger to corporations and individual schoolchildren of all ages. Here are some of the things they gave:

- 40,000 pounds of soap and toothpaste
- 340,000 pounds of lemonade
- 1,720 pounds of hard candy
- 835 pounds of Kool-Aid
- 25,000 paperback books
- 12,000 golf balls
- 250,000 packages of Fritos
- 47 tons of mixed fruit juices
- 40,000 disposable cameras
- 5,000 "Blockhead" games

• probably the most unusual item was the cosmetic lotion "Skin-So-Soft," which turned out to be an excellent insect repellent.

When the United States military began sending troops to the Middle East, they asked the Hershey Foods Corporation (the company that makes Hershey's candy bars) to invent a chocolate bar that would not melt in the desert sun. That way, American soldiers could have chocolate during the summer in the Middle East and not worry about it melting in their pockets. Hershey Foods called this the "Desert Bar." They sent a total of 894,000 of these bars to the American troops during the Gulf War. (Hershey Foods did not donate but sold these chocolate bars to the military.)

Chapter 6

The End of War

It's important to understand not just the beginning and middle of war but also the end of war. Peace is very fragile. It's sometimes more difficult to make than war. Franklin D. Roosevelt, who was president (and commander in chief) during World War II, said, "More than an end to war, we want an end to the beginnings of war."

How does a war end?

One side might decide to hold up a white flag (meaning "I give up"), put down their weapons, and surrender, or both sides might agree to stop fighting. When this happens, the highest-ranking generals of both sides send messages back and forth. They agree to stop shooting and to talk. This is called a cease-fire. The side that is winning will tell the side that is losing what it must do to stop the war officially. The generals become diplomats and negotiate. First, the generals talk to their commanders in chief to find out what is okay and what isn't okay. They decide on special conditions and the terms for peace. They discuss all the details and then write up a formal document listing what everyone agrees to do.

Those involved in the war usually agree to exchange prisoners, and agreements are made to assure that everyone gets home safely. They discuss what happens to the soldiers and equipment left on the battlefield. They also discuss what promises the losing side will make to make sure that the fighting does not begin again. Finally, the winning side must decide what kind of relationship it will have with the losing side in the future. Sometimes the work involved in this effort is nearly as hard as fighting an actual war.

After a cease-fire, can both sides go home?

It depends. Usually, the two sides in a war have a lot to work out. They have to figure out if anyone should be made to pay for things that were destroyed. They have to figure out if the boundaries between the nations at war should be changed or stay the same. They have to figure out what to do with refugees (people whose lives were completely changed by the war, whose homes, lands, schools, and businesses were destroyed and who have no place to go). They try to figure out how to keep peace and get things back to normal. The diplomats start talking again, too.

When do the soldiers get to come home?

Soldiers have to wait for orders from the senior officers before they can pack up their stuff and be sent home. Just as it takes time to get ready for a war, set up camps, and send over the troops, it also takes time to leave. The armed forces have to pack up everything and get all their equipment (including the tanks and missile launchers) home, too. Some soldiers have to "mop up" the mess. There are also some dangerous jobs still to do, like finding and destroying unexploded mines. Gradually, most of the troops are sent home. Some will stay to help keep the peace.

What about all the destruction that was done in Kuwait, Saudi Arabia, Israel, and Iraq during the Persian Gulf War?

The people and the leaders of these nations will rebuild their countries with the help of their allies. There is a lot of hard work to do. Kuwait City (the capital of Kuwait) and Baghdad (the capital of Iraq) and the other cities in Kuwait and Iraq are a wreck. Engineers will have to rebuild the buildings, bridges, roads, and houses that were smashed by bombs and missiles. The Kuwaiti oil fields that are on fire will take many years to put out. The oil spill and other pollution caused by the war need attention. The air pollution caused by the burning oil fields is said to be many hundreds of'times worse than the levels of pollution found in the most polluted areas of the world. The region's animals, including fish and many species of dolphins, whales, and sea birds, are at risk.

Why does the United States get involved with other people's problems?

That's a complicated question with many answers. Some people don't think we should get involved with other nations' fights. But the United States is the wealthiest and strongest nation in the world. Sometimes we get involved with other countries just because we want to help them. Sometimes we want something in return for helping. When we went to war with Iraq, for example, we wanted to destroy Saddam Hussein's military power *and* we wanted to make sure we, and the rest of the world, could always buy oil from Kuwait at a fair price. Sometimes other countries want our help and ask for it. In

World War II, the United States helped Britain and France fight Germany. Our allies were grateful. Sometimes countries get mad when we interfere.

What happens when peace finally comes after a war?

The people who were in the war will probably be most interested in getting back to living their lives. There will be parades and welcome-home celebrations for the soldiers. The generals will give some men and women promotions and medals. The president might decide to give the generals promotions and medals. The United Nations goes to work to keep the peace. People give thanks for the safe return of the soldiers and hope and pray that war will not happen again.

Will there ever be peace in the world?

Let's hope so. Maybe if the grown-ups let the kids run everything for a day. . . . A poet named Carl Sandburg once wrote, "Sometime they'll give a war and nobody will come."

What can we do to prevent war?

Peace is not just the end of war. It's a full-time job. We should enjoy every minute of it. And we should also try to solve the problems that make people want to go to war. If we can help reduce the poverty, fear, and hatred in the world, we will make peace a reality.

"Peace" in 25 Languages

Language	Peace
Greek:	iri'ni
Arabic:	salam
Turkish:	sulh
Hebrew:	shalom
Yiddish:	sholim
French:	paix
Spanish:	paz
Portugese:	paz
Italian:	pace
German:	Friedon
Dutch:	vrede
Danish:	fred
Swedish:	fred
Norwegian:	fred
Finnish:	ruaha
Russian:	mir
Serbo-Croatian:	mir
Rumanian:	pace
Polish:	pokój
Czech:	mir
Hungarian:	béke
Indonesian:	perdamaian
Esperanto:	paco
Japanese:	heiwa
Swahili:	amani

Appendix: What You Can Do

War is not something that just happens to people. People make war happen. Many people also work to make war *not* happen. They do this by having peace marches, signing petitions, writing letters to the president and to people in Congress, and joining organizations that work toward world peace. So there *are* things you yourself can do if you want to express your feelings about war. Here are some suggestions:

1) Write a letter to the president of the United States and tell him what you think about war. His address is:

> 1600 Pennsylvania Avenue N.W.
> Washington, D.C. 20500

He might even write you back!

2) Write a letter to a congressperson from your state. Your opinions are important to them because they have been elected to represent *you* (meaning they have been sent to Washington, D.C., to make laws that express the opinions of people in your state about certain issues, like war). Where you send your let-

ter depends on whether the congressperson you are writing to is in the House of Representatives or in the Senate. You can find out who the representatives for your state are by asking your parents or by calling the League of Women Voters (their number is in the phone book). Here are the addresses to write to:

> The Honorable _____
> U.S. House of Representatives
> Washington, D.C. 20515

> The Honorable _____
> U.S. Senate
> Washington, D.C. 20510

3) Join or find out about kids' organizations that deal with issues of war and peace. You can become politically involved and discuss your views with other kids. Several organizations are:

Kids Meeting Kids
380 Riverside Drive, Box 8-H
New York, N.Y. 10025

This is an organization in which kids get together to talk about peace in the world. Even though the group is based in New York, you don't have to live there to be a part of it.

WHAT YOU CAN DO

You can write or call to find out about activities going on in other places. Here are some of the things the organization offers:

• political activities—during the Persian Gulf War, kids from this group had meetings with the secretary general of the United Nations and Iraqi officials, and they also went to the United Nations building.

• international pen pals—write to another child halfway around the world and find out how he or she feels about war and peace and everything else!

• international meetings with other kids where you talk about the needs and rights of children.

The telephone number for Kids Meeting Kids is (212) 662-2327. You can call to find out more information.

Children's Creative Response to Conflict
Fellowship of Reconciliation
P.O. Box 271
Nyack, N.Y. 10960

Their telephone number is (914) 358-4601.

If you write or call this organization, they will send you a book on how to solve problems creatively, without fighting. (It might give you some more answers to the question, "How do you keep a cat and a dog from fighting?")

Educators for Social Responsibility
475 Riverside Drive, Rm. 450
New York, N.Y. 10115

This organization has a program called "Resolving Conflict Creatively," which it teaches in New York City public schools. If you are interested in learning about this program, or if you want to find out about other peace organizations, or if you just have general questions about war and peace, you can send for all sorts of information and reading material. They encourage people to call and will be glad to help you in whatever way they can.

4) Find out about other peace organizations in your city or town. They would be happy to have you involved.

5) Talk about these issues with your friends. You will probably find that you all have similar questions, and it often helps to share them.

Glossary

Armored personnel carrier—a light armored vehicle used to transport infantry on the battlefield.

Arms— military weapons.

Artillery—large guns or cannons which can be either pulled or driven. They can fire large quantities of heavy explosive shells.

Bomb shelter— a room built underground to protect citizens from airplane bombing overhead.

Bunker—a protective concrete and steel shelter on a battlefield used to protect people and equipment from bombing.

Cease-fire—a temporary stopping of warfare agreed to by both sides.

Chemical warfare—fighting with weapons, such as bombs, missiles, and artillery shells, that contain deadly chemicals inside them. When these weapons explode, they let out poisonous gases which can kill huge numbers of people. Often, citizens are given gas masks during wartime as a precautionary measure, so they will not breathe in the chemicals if they are used.

Diplomat—a representative of a country who speaks to representatives of other countries. Diplomats try to prevent war through verbal negotiations.

WHAT IS WAR? WHAT IS PEACE?

Embargo—a rule that forbids ships, planes, trucks, and other vehicles carrying supplies from entering or leaving a country. Used against countries in order to make their survival difficult.

Guided missile—a rocket that heads for a specific target and destroys it upon impact. It can be sent from the ground, a ship, or a plane.

Home front—refers to the area (the home country) of civilian activity during war.

Infantry— the part of an army that fights on foot.

Logistics—the complicated process of moving, supplying, and housing soldiers.

Mine—an explosive object, hidden in either the ground or the sea, which destroys anything that touches it.

Negotiation—the process of talking with someone in order to reach an agreement on a particular issue. Countries try to avoid war by negotiating with each other.

Occupation—when one country has invaded another country and has taken over the government, claiming that the invading country is now their own.

Peace—freedom from war, fighting, and disagreement. What comes at the end of a war.

Prisoner of war—a soldier captured by the opposing side during a war (known as a POW). According to the rules of war, a POW must be treated well by his or her captors.

Reparations—payments made by a defeated country to a winning country for damage done during the war, such as destroyed property, stolen goods, and people wounded or killed.

Retreat—the withdrawal of troops from a certain position, usually because they are forced back by the enemy.

Sortie—an attack by a single military airplane against a target.

Strategy—the science of large-scale military planning.

Surrender—when an army gives up and lays down its weapons.

Tactics—the arrangement of troops, tanks, ships, and planes within the area of battle, and how they are used in the fight.

Tank—a heavily armored, tracked vehicle with a very large cannon. The first ones were used in World War II.

Trench— a long, narrow ditch dug in the earth by soldiers to protect themselves from enemy gun- and artillery fire.

WHAT IS WAR? WHAT IS PEACE?

United Nations—the international organization of nations dedicated to solving world problems and seeking world peace. Its headquarters—where the diplomats from all the member nations get together to talk—are in New York City.

Victory—final and complete success in defeating the enemy. It usually occurs as the outcome of an important battle, and marks the end of a war.

Yellow ribbon—a symbol used in the United States to remind Americans of U.S. troops serving in a war. It has been used since the Civil War in the 1860's.

INDEX

INDEX

ABOUT THE CONTRIBUTORS

RICHARD RABINOWITZ is a historian and educator with a special interest in programs for children. He has written many articles and books about American history. As president of American History Workshop, he has also created museums and television programs about the people and places of the United States. He has been reading history books since he was in elementary school in New York City. He has a Ph.D. in the History of American Civilization from Harvard University and has been a college teacher in Massachusetts, New York, and California.

PAUL MEISEL graduated from the Yale School of Art and worked as an art director before becoming a full-time illustrator. He is a frequent contributor to the *New York Times* and illustrator of *Mr. Bubble Gum*, *Mr. Monster*, and the best-selling Camelot World book *A Kid's Guide to How to Save the Planet*.

The author would like to acknowledge the help of the children in the following schools: The Bolles School in Jacksonville, Florida, and Waverly Elementary School in Frederick, Maryland; their teachers, Mrs. Nancy Ehlert and Mrs. Edythe McDannell; the Defense Personnel Support Center; Secretary of the Army for Public Affairs; Navy's Office of Information; Marine's Division of Public Affairs; Secretary of the Air Force Office of Public Affairs; and his colleagues in this project: Jeffrey Eger, Laurie Mittenthal, Joan Tally, Lisbeth Mark, Gillian Bucky, and our friends at BPVP.

Photo Credits: Pages 3, 13, 17, 19, 33, 39, 69, 71, 73, 80, 91, courtesy AP/Wide World Photos; pages 24, 60, from *The American Revolution Picture Book*, a Dover Picture Archive Series; pages 31, 75, courtesy U.S. Defense Department; page 35, photograph by Alexander Gardner, courtesy Library of Congress; page 43, photograph by Timothy H. O'Sullivan or Alexander Gardner, courtesy Library of Congress; page 48, courtesy General Dynamics; page 52, courtesy Robert Hunt Library; page 54, courtesy Newport News Shipbuilding; pages 65, 95, courtesy Imperial War Museum.